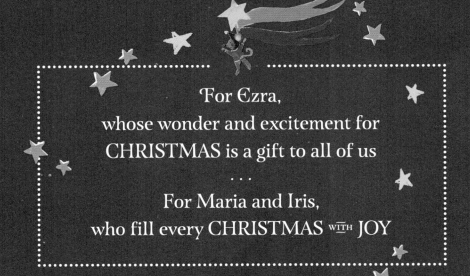

For Ezra,
whose wonder and excitement for
CHRISTMAS is a gift to all of us
. . .
For Maria and Iris,
who fill every CHRISTMAS WITH JOY

The Library of Congress catalog record is available at https://lccn.loc.gov/2019047982.

ISBN 978-0-525-65414-8
eBook ISBN 978-0-525-65415-5

Printed in the United States of America

Cover design by Jessie Kaye

10 9 8 7 6 5 4 3 2 1

ALL THE COLORS OF
Christmas

MATTHEW PAUL TURNER

Bestselling Author of *When I Pray for You*

Illustrated by Gillian Gamble

CONVERGENT

Christmas is RED.

It's a shiny new sled.

It's candy canes
and toy-store lanes.

It's sprinkles on sweet bread.

It's packages with bows
and Rudolph's bright red nose.

It's pictures drawn
and dressed-up lawns.

It's warm mittens
when it snows.

It's the drummer boy's drum,

his "pah rum pah pum pum."

It's Santa Claus
and cranberry sauce.

It's apples, pears, and plums,

It's presents that we send
to family and to friends.

It's jolly cards
and merry hearts.

Yes, Christmas is RED.

Christmas is GREEN.

It's an evergreen scene.

It's holly sprigs
and mistletoe twigs.

It's emerald lights agleam.

It's garland on rails and pine-needled trails.

It's winter boots
and funny elf suits.

It's that ole Mr. Grinch tale.

It's Granny Smith pies
and plaid bow ties.

It's fresh potpourri
that smells Christmassy.

It's stockings hung high.

It's tinsel on trees
and grass iced by freeze.

It's Christmas tree balls
and artwork on walls.

Yes, Christmas is GREEN.

Christmas is GOLD.

It's bright ribbon unrolled.

It's jingling bells
and warm, yummy smells.

It's heirlooms YOU ARE NOT ALLOWED TO HOLD.

It's dancers all tapping among holiday trappings.

It's nutcracker crowns
and Christmas Eve gowns.

It's glittery gift wrapping.

It's a big turkey roast
and walnuts you toast.

It's crackling fires
and glorious choirs.

It's an ornament you love most.

It's kids shouting "Behold!"
wearing halos and robes.

It's treetop stars
and old church bazaars.

Yes, Christmas is GOLD.

Christmas is BLUE.

It's a winter sky's hue.

It's flannel sheets
and shaped cookie treats.

It's a lake frozen through.

It's big puffy coats and huge parade floats.

It's juniper trees
and blue spruce wreaths.

It's writing Santa notes.

It's a sweater Mama knit,
stretched yet still fits.

It's turquoise lights
in the darkest of nights.

It's a snowman's outfit.

It's memories, old and new,
of loved ones gone too soon.

It's an Elvis song
and nights growing long.

Yes, Christmas is BLUE.

Christmas is WHITE.

It's warm candlelight.

It's mountaintops
and small fancy shops.

It's turtledoves in flight.

It's December snowstorms
and blankets so warm.

It's angel wings
and the song that we sing
about our dream for Christmas morn.

It's sleigh rides through snow
and tea lights that glow.

It's North Pole tales
and frosty exhales.

It's cocoa with marshmallows.

It's a star shining bright
on the holiest of nights.

It's powdered cakes
and paper snowflakes.

Yes, Christmas is WHITE.

Christmas is BROWN.

It's pine cones scattered round.

It's caramel corn
and copper French horns.

It's winter's frozen ground.

It's firewood piled high
and reindeer that fly.

It's cinnamon sweets
and gingerbread treats.

It's homemade pecan pie.

It's a cradle soft with hay
and a donkey's gentle bray.

It's God within
a baby's skin

on that very first Christmas Day.

It's shepherds kneeling down
and wise ones gathered round.

It's Mary's sigh
and Jesus's cry.

Yes, Christmas is BROWN.

Christmas is YOU!

It's your own unique hue.

It's your wondrous gleam
and your bedtime dreams.

You color each Christmas anew.

It's your tinsel and flair and the gifts that you share.

It's your jingling smile
and your "fa la la" style.

It's how you love and you care

It's the songs that you sing
and the light that you bring.

It's your heartfelt compassion
and your hope put in action.

It's your thrill for the little things.

It's your love for what's true.

It's the good that you do.

You're a part of the story,
the joy and the glory.

Yes, Christmas is YOU.